Mummies

by David Orme

Rans⬤m

Trailblazers

Mummies
by David Orme
Educational consultant: Helen Bird

Illustrated by Elisa Huber and Cyber Media (India) Ltd.

Published by Ransom Publishing Ltd.
Rose Cottage, Howe Hill, Watlington, Oxon. OX49 5HB
www.ransom.co.uk

ISBN   184167 427 3
           978 184167 427 8

First published in 2006

Illustrations copyright © 2006 Elisa Huber and Ransom Publishing Ltd.
Photograph of Howard Carter courtesy Uni Bonn. Photograph of the ice man
courtesy AFP/Getty Images.

Every effort has been made to locate all copyright holders of material used in this
book. If any errors or omissions have occurred, corrections will be made in future
editions of this book.

A CIP catalogue record of this book is available from the British Library.

The rights of David Orme to be identified as the author and of Elisa Huber and Cyber
Media (India) Ltd. to be identified as the illustrators of this Work have been asserted by
them in accordance with sections 77 and 78 of the Copyright, Design and Patents Act
1988.

Printed in China through Colorcraft Ltd., Hong Kong.

Mummies

Contents

Mummies

Get the facts

What is a mummy?

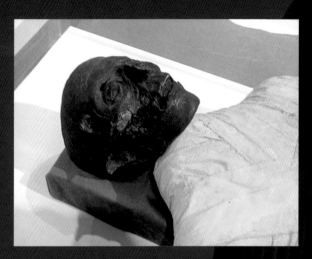

Mummies are dead bodies.

The bodies are wrapped in strips of cloth.

Sometimes the wrapped body is put in a special box.

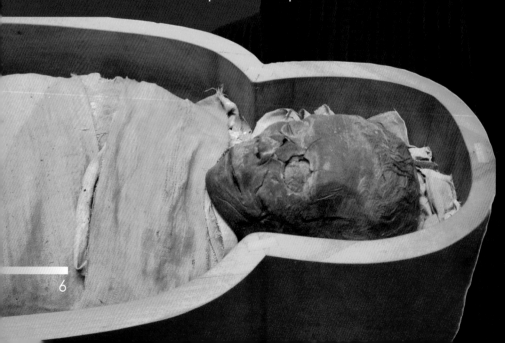

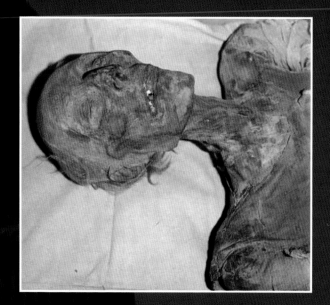

This mummy has been unwrapped.

Not all mummies are people. The ancient Egyptians made mummies from the bodies of cats, crocodiles, apes and cows!

This is a cat mummy.

Where do they come from?

Most mummies in our museums have come from Egypt.

This is not the only country where we find mummies.

This mummy came from South America.

This mummy was found
in the Swiss Alps, near
to the border with Italy.
He has been named
'The Ice Man'.

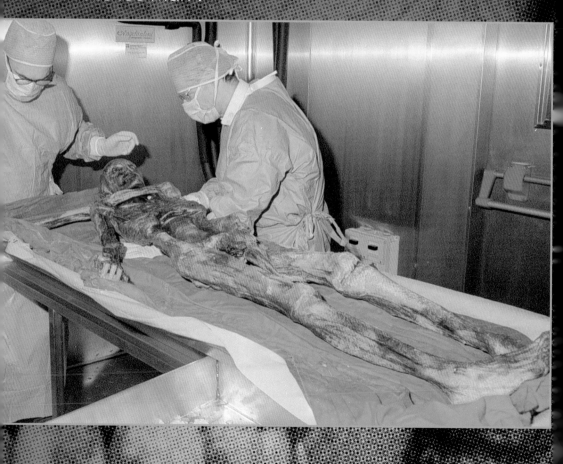

How are mummies made?

Some mummies, like the Ice Man, just happen naturally.

Scientists think he died in the mountains. His body was frozen and kept in the ice for thousands of years.

The Egyptians made their mummies by cutting out the insides of the body and packing the space with a sort of salt called **Natron**.

Most mummies are found in very dry places.

They kept all the inside parts, like the heart, in special jars.

Then the body was tightly wrapped in bandages.

Treasure

Scientists like to study all old mummies, but Egyptian mummies are special.

Sometimes these mummies were buried in boxes made of gold.

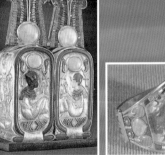

They had jewels buried with them.

The Egyptian kings were buried with things they owned when they were alive.

This Egyptian king was called Tutankhamen.

He is the most famous mummy ever found.

A man called Howard Carter found his tomb in 1922.

There was more treasure in this tomb than had ever been found with a mummy before.

13

The mummy's curse

Some people think that it is bad luck to dig up a mummy.

These people say that when Howard Carter found Tutankhamen's tomb, some of the people who were with him died soon after.

Howard Carter and
Lord Carnarvon

Lord Carnarvon
was one of these.
He was the man
who paid Howard
Carter to do the
digging.

Other people say that
some mummies can
come back to life.

What do you think?

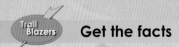

Mummies in museums

Some famous mummies are kept in museums.

Tutankhamen was kept in his tomb for a long time. Now he is in a museum.

Scientists like to find out what is inside the cloth wrapping. They used to have to unwrap the mummies, but now they can use X-rays to see inside.

In 1974 the mummy of the king Rameses II was flown to Paris.

Scientists wanted to find out more about him.

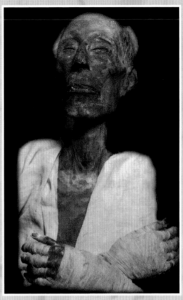

He had to have his own passport. The passport said his job was "King (deceased)" which means dead King!

Before museums began to make collections of mummies, some people bought them to keep in their own homes.

Would you like a mummy in your house?

The

Walking

Horror

Chapter 1:
Work experience

Ethan loved history. He thought it was great when the head of the town museum said he could do his work experience there.

The museum had a great collection of Egyptian mummies. Ethan hoped he could work in the room where they kept the mummies.

But this didn't happen. On his first day, he was told to make the tea and do the washing up!

Carrie and Dan worked at the museum. They were pleased when Ethan came to do work experience. It meant they didn't have to make the tea and do the washing up.

Carrie and Dan didn't work very hard. They were going out together. Ethan caught them once kissing in the office. After a while having Ethan hanging round got on their nerves.

Chapter 2:
The curse

Ethan kept on about the mummies.

"I want to look after them," he said.

"They don't need looking after. They're dead! They just lie there," said Dan.

The head of the museum said they must not be touched. Ethan was fed up.

"We've got to do something about that kid," said Carrie to Dan. "He's always hanging round the place."

"I know," said Dan. "Let's do the old mummy's curse thing."

They called Ethan up to where the mummies were.

"Have you been told about the curse?" Dan asked him.

Ethan didn't believe Dan.

"What does the curse say?"

"Sometimes a mummy comes to life and starts touching people. They die a horrible death!"

Carrie started giggling. She couldn't help it.

"You won't catch me with that old rubbish," Ethan said.

Chapter 3:
The plan

That wasn't the end of the plan. The next morning, Dan got Carrie to wrap him up in bandages.

"Send Ethan to the Mummy Room when he gets here," he said. "I'll hide in that dark corner. Then I'll do my famous mummy walk."

He stuck his arms out and started walking around like a mummy from a horror film.

When Ethan arrived, Carrie told him what to do. She tried not to laugh.

"You've got to go up to the Mummy Room and sweep it," she said. "Don't forget the curse!"

"Huh! You won't catch me with that stupid story," said Ethan.

He set off to the Mummy Room with a broom. Carrie followed him. She wanted to see what would happen.

Chapter 4:
The touch of death

Ethan started sweeping the floor, though it wasn't very dirty. Suddenly, he heard a moaning noise from the dark corner. A bandaged, man-shaped thing came staggering out towards him. Ethan could hear Carrie giggling outside.

"Dan, that's stupid," said Ethan. "You're not scaring me."

But the mummy came on and on. It went out of the room and grabbed Carrie's arm.

"Ow, that hurt!" said Carrie.

Then Dan arrived.

"Sorry, Carrie. The boss saw me. He gave me a right telling off."

Carrie and Ethan stared at him.

"Dan! Is that really you?" said Ethan.

"Of course it's me!"

"So who is THAT?" he said, pointing to the bandaged thing staggering down the corridor.

Carrie screamed.

"It touched me!"

She stared at her arm, where the flesh was beginning to go rotten and peel away.

Mummies word check

ancient	museum
bandages	natron
believe	owned
border	packing
buried	Paris
collections	passport
crocodiles	Rameses
country	rotten
curse	rubbish
deceased	scientists
Egypt	South America
Egyptian	staggering
famous	stared
giggling	Swiss Alps
history	treasure
horrible	Tutankhamen
horror	wrap
Italy	wrapped
moaning	wrapping
mountains	work experience
mummy	X-rays
mummies	